THE INCLUSIVE EVENT PLANNER

A Quick Guide to Planning Sober-Friendly Conferences That Boost Attendance.

By Laura Nelson

© 2024 Laura Nelson

Imagine walking into a room filled with industry leaders, eager professionals, and potential collaborators, only to feel like an outsider because the social glue that binds everyone together is something you've chosen to avoid—alcohol. Countless professionals find themselves on the margins of networking events, not because they lack the desire to connect, but because the atmosphere is centered around something that excludes them. This book isn't just about providing an alternative; it's about revolutionizing the way we think about professional conferences, gatherings and meetings. When creating events, the goal is to where everyone, regardless of their choices, can feel included, connected, and truly valued. Whether you're an event planner looking to boost attendance or a meeting planner looking to make sure everyone attending your meeting feels included and leaves filled up, this book is your guide to making it happen.

Welcome to The Inclusive Event Planner: A Quick Guide to Planning Sober-Friendly Conferences That Boost Attendance.

Let me start by being upfront with you—I'm not a meeting planner, nor have I ever overseen organizing large conferences. So, you might be wondering, why should you listen to me? What makes my perspective on this topic worth considering? Well, let me share a bit about my journey and why I'm so passionate about creating more inclusive conferences, especially for those who choose not to drink. My experience comes from a different angle, one that you might not have thought about before but could make all the difference in how your events are perceived and experienced.

I've spent over a decade as a professional speaker, attending and presenting at hundreds of conferences. I've seen it all—the good, the bad, and the downright awful. I've been on both sides of the "bar," so to speak. For most of my speaking career, I was a drinker. I know firsthand how the culture of conferences can revolve around alcohol, from the moment you step into the airport to when you finally check out of the hotel.

Traveling and speaking became integral to my career, and along with them, so did drinking. If you've spent any time in an industry where travel, conferences, after-hours events, and networking are the norm, you're likely familiar with the routine. It's almost an unspoken expectation that these activities go together, making it easy for drinking to become a regular part of the job.

This book isn't just for event planners; it's also for HR professionals or anyone looking to make their meetings and company events more inclusive. Whether you're organizing a large conference or a small team-building event, understanding how to create environments where everyone feels welcome—including those who choose not to drink—is crucial. My perspective, shaped by years of experience and personal growth, offers insights that can help you rethink how you plan your next event, ensuring it's an experience where all attendees feel valued and included.

Not everyone reading this will have had the same experience, so let me paint a picture of what this can look like for some, including myself. It often starts innocently enough, but over the years, it can become a significant issue for many. You arrive at the airport, and suddenly, time feels irrelevant—a mimosa in the morning or a beer before takeoff becomes just another part of the travel routine. If you look around any airport, you'll see bars packed with people drinking at all hours of the day. As you accumulate more travel miles, upgrades to business class become frequent, and with them comes the free-flowing wine. After landing, it's straight to the conference hotel, and within minutes of checking in, you're at the hotel bar, joining colleagues who have flown in from all over. And this is all just the warm-up to the actual conference.

I don't need to describe the rest of the conference experience to you, a seasoned planner. Attendees overindulge in food, drink too much, and rarely step outside to get fresh air before heading home. It's an endless cycle that, for many, becomes the norm. For me, it became a problem.

It was much like living a double life. I would try to be healthy, not drink, work out and eat well at home for a few days and then back on the road to the next conference where, like Groundhog Day, we did the same thing just in a different hotel or conference center in a different city.

In January 2020, after years of living this way, I woke up one day and decided I had to stop drinking. Conveniently—or perhaps serendipitously—the world shut down about a month and a half later, giving me the chance to quietly and privately get sober at home. No more conferences, no more airport bars, and no more hotel gatherings. It was just me, at home, learning how to navigate life without alcohol. With a lot of newly discovered free time, I dove deep into understanding alcohol, addiction, and how we can retrain our brains. I was fortunate enough to not only learn but to become a certified coach with the This Naked Mind Institute, a program designed to help people reframe their relationship with alcohol and other addictions using Affective Liminal Psychology.

My mission now goes beyond one-on-one coaching; I aim to educate and inspire from the stage, transforming the way meetings and conferences are designed so that people don't feel so alone. Overcoming an addiction is challenging enough, and I'm on a mission to help others understand that they don't have to hit rock bottom to make a change—they're not alone in their journey. Through my work, I want to create environments where people can connect meaningfully, without the pressure of alcohol, and where making sober decisions feels not only accepted but celebrated as a normal and empowering choice.

After what was supposed to be a brief three-month pause that turned into three years, the world finally began to open up, and conferences resumed. I returned to speaking, but this time, everything looked different. Experiencing events as a non-drinker was nothing short of eye-opening. I spent the next year navigating airports, hotel lobbies, bars, and conference happy hours, all while learning to handle the subtle, yet pervasive peer pressure that most people don't even realize exists—until they stop drinking.

Throughout this new journey, I discovered plenty of ways to successfully navigate "life" without alcohol. In airports, I traded the bar scene for coffee shops and shopping. When I arrived at hotel lobbies, I would politely wave to colleagues gathered in the bar and head up to my room to enjoy a chocolate treat I had picked up at check-in, followed by a restful night's sleep. Even when I did choose to join friends in the bar, there were usually good options available for me, like a refreshing mojito sans alcohol or an alcohol-free beer.

The real challenge for me emerged once the conference officially kicked off and the typical happy hour or evening events began. As the black bars were rolled in, the usual options were laid out: beer, wine, soda, and, at more upscale events, mixed drinks. Standing in line with peers and colleagues, I would feel a wave of anxiety wash over me as I faced the inevitable question of what to order:

1. Should I "fake" drinking by ordering a club soda with lime? Carrying around a drink might make it look like I'm fitting in, but it only deepened my sense of isolation, making me feel like the only one who wasn't, or couldn't be, part of the crowd.
2. Should I openly admit that I don't drink and brace myself for the inevitable barrage of questions: "Are you pregnant?" "Why don't you drink?"
3. Or should I deal with the peer pressure: "Come on, just have one!" These questions weren't just awkward—they were sometimes downright triggering, especially for someone who had made a conscious choice to avoid alcohol.

What I also noticed, after attending several of these events, was how the atmosphere started to shift after about 30 minutes. Conversations became more difficult as people began to lose focus or repeat themselves after their second drink. The noise level in the room would rise, making it increasingly challenging to hear or be heard. Now that I no longer drank, I found myself with less patience for this kind of interaction, knowing that many of these exchanges would likely be forgotten by morning. Often, I would quietly slip away to my hotel room much earlier than I ever did before 2020.

It got me thinking—if I'm feeling this way, how many others are too? And if networking is supposed to be the primary reason for attending these conferences, why am I even here if I'm heading back to my room early every night?

The issue I felt had a two-part approach. The first step was to start a community of like-minded individuals, and the second was to tackle the cultural issues of meetings that have been going on forever—issues that often make those who choose sobriety feel excluded. This is why I wrote this book. It seems that while society is moving forward in many ways, meetings and conferences have often remained stuck in outdated practices that don't cater to everyone. It's time to change that.

This realization led me to co-found Sober Life Rocks, a community of professionals who celebrate and honor sober choices. We designed our logo as a puzzle piece, symbolizing the final, crucial element of life improvement that many of us discovered when we chose sobriety. The puzzle piece also represents the connection we share with others who have made similar choices—each of us fitting together to form a supportive network where everyone has a place.

We give this puzzle piece to all our members to wear at events and conferences. By wearing it, our members can easily identify one another in a crowd, creating an instant connection and a sense of belonging. It's a subtle yet powerful way to ensure that no one feels isolated or out of place. Instead, they can confidently engage in the event, knowing they are part of a larger community that honors and supports their choices.

The second part of this approach is to address and change the long-standing cultural issues in meeting and event planning. Many of these practices have gone unchallenged for years, but you can't fix what you don't know is broken. I hope this book will provide you with some valuable insights into these areas, helping you to create more inclusive and welcoming environments at your events. Together, we can reshape the way conferences are experienced, ensuring that they are places where everyone feels welcome, connected, and valued.

But this isn't just about inclusivity; it's about the future of conferences and company events themselves. Meeting attendance is on the decline, and as a speaker, I want to ensure that I'm speaking to full rooms for years to come. Boosting attendance is crucial for all of us who believe in the value of professional gatherings, including HR professionals who are responsible for fostering team unity and engagement within their organizations. Unfortunately, many conferences and corporate events are attempting to counter this decline by doubling down on alcohol as a main attraction. We're seeing extended happy hours on exhibit hall floors, wine tasting events, and other alcohol-focused activities. However, these strategies aren't resonating with those who are seeking genuine connections and meaningful networking experiences.

It's time to rethink how we engage attendees and create environments that truly foster the connections people are seeking. This book is about helping you do just that—whether you're an event planner or an HR professional—by crafting events that welcome everyone, regardless of their drinking preferences, and making sure no one feels left out or alone. Together, we can build a future where events are more inclusive, engaging, and successful for all involved.

In this book, I'm not just going to give you a list of "how-tos"; I'm going to share real-life examples of conferences I have attended that have done things well and those that have missed the mark. My goal is to help you create events where everyone feels welcome, included, and fulfilled—where attendees leave not feeling depleted or like they've missed out but rather energized, connected, and glad they came.

So, let's get started. Together, we can reimagine the way conferences are done and ensure that every attendee leaves feeling truly filled up.

About The Author

Laura Nelson is a dynamic entrepreneur, international speaker, author, and a trailblazer in the dental industry, but her most passionate mission is to advocate for a sober lifestyle. As a co-founder of Sober Life Rocks, Laura is committed to making professional environments more inclusive and supportive for individuals who choose to make sober choices or live a sober life. Her initiative promotes encouraging industry events and professionals to embrace healthier choices and create welcoming spaces for everyone—no matter what is in their cup.

Laura's dedication to sober living is not just a personal choice; it reflects her belief that a healthy lifestyle leads to greater success and fulfillment both personally and professionally. By normalizing sober choices at industry gatherings, she aims to dismantle the stigma around sobriety and foster a culture of acceptance and support. Through Sober Life Rocks, Laura inspires others to prioritize their well-being and find joy in social settings without alcohol.

In addition to her advocacy work, Laura is the founder of Front Office Rocks, a groundbreaking online training platform that has transformed the way dental front office staff are educated. Her commitment to enhancing patient care and practice management is complemented by her efforts to promote a healthier, more inclusive dental community.

Laura's vision is clear: a world where professionals can feel included and no one cares what's in your cup. Join her as she shares her journey, insights, and experiences, inspiring others to embrace sober living while transforming professional event space. Through her work, Laura is not just changing the narrative; she's creating a movement that celebrates wellness, community, and the power of choice.

TABLE OF CONTENTS:

WHY SOBER FRIENDLY? Understanding the demand for inclusive events..1

MORE THAN A DRINK: The Lasting Benefits of Sober-Inclusive Conferences...9

IDENTIFYING YOUR AUDIENCE: Why You Have Not Recognized This Audience Before...18

RAISING THE BAR: The Crucial Role of Bars and Bartenders in Shaping Event Atmosphere 24

STRATEGIC PARTNERSHIPS: Planning a Sober-Friendly Event with Venue Collaboration and Alcohol-Free Brand Integration..51

PLANNING THE PERFECT VENUE: Making Spaces that Support Inclusivity 59

CREATIVE PROGRAMMING: Engaging Activities That Don't Eliminate Alcohol but Also Don't Revolve Around Alcohol .. 66

MARKETING YOUR EVENT: Attracting Attendees to your Sober-Friendly event... 75

CREATING A WELCOMING ENVIRONMENT: Tips to Make It Easier for Attendees to Feel Included Before They Even Arrive... 84

THE FUTURE OF EVENT PLANNING: Trends in Inclusivity and Sober Events.. 89

YOUR NEXT STEPS: Putting It All Together for a Successful Conference 96

Chapter 1

WHY SOBER FRIENDLY?
Understanding the demand for inclusive events

In today's dynamic and diverse professional world, inclusivity in event planning has become more than just a buzzword—it's a necessity. But what does it really mean to create an inclusive event? It's about more than just ticking off boxes on a checklist. True inclusivity is about actively embracing diversity, creating environments that cater to the wide range of needs, preferences, and lifestyles of all attendees. This is especially crucial for HR professionals who are tasked with creating environments that foster unity and engagement within their teams. One of the most pressing areas where this inclusivity is being demanded is in the realm of sober-friendly spaces.

The landscape of social interaction is changing. More and more, people are seeking out environments where they feel genuinely welcome, respected, and comfortable—regardless of whether they choose to drink alcohol. This shift isn't merely about catering to a minority; it's about recognizing that a broad spectrum of attendees, including employees at corporate events, may prefer an atmosphere that doesn't revolve around alcohol. By doing so, event planners and HR professionals can significantly enhance both attendance and participant satisfaction, making their events stand out in a crowded field.

We've already seen a similar shift when it comes to dietary needs. Gone are the days when the only options at events were meat and potatoes. Today, offering gluten-free, vegan, or allergen-free options is the norm, and attendees expect the same level of consideration when it comes to alcohol-free choices. This is not just about serving up some soda water; it's about curating an environment where everyone, regardless of their drinking habits, can feel included and engaged.

In today's digital age, much of the information people seek can easily be found online, so the real reason they attend events is to be involved and connect with others. When attendees feel that their needs are being addressed, they are far more likely to participate fully and engage with the event. This leads to more active involvement, meaningful networking, and a stronger positive experience overall. Sober-friendly events, in particular, help create an environment where the focus shifts from drinking to fostering genuine connections and interactions—the true purpose of gathering in person.

Let's take a closer look at why sober-friendly environments are becoming increasingly important. In professional settings, where networking often involves social drinking, non-drinkers frequently find themselves on the sidelines, feeling awkward or excluded. This isn't just a matter of personal choice; it's about broader issues like health, cultural values, and lifestyle preferences. The growing demand for sober-friendly spaces reflects a deeper need for events that respect and cater to diverse attendee needs.

Picture this: you're at a conference or a corporate event where the primary interactions happen over cocktails, and every conversation seems to revolve around what's in your glass. For those who choose not to drink, this can be an isolating experience. They might stick around for the early part of the evening but quietly retreat as the night wears on. Some might even skip these events entirely, feeling that the environment isn't designed with them in mind.

Moreover, the emphasis on alcohol at many events overlooks the wide range of reasons someone might choose not to drink—be it health concerns, personal well-being, religious beliefs, or simply a preference for sobriety. Imagine being a professional who abstains from alcohol and walking into a networking event centered around a wine tasting. Your choice to abstain suddenly sets you apart, and with few alternative options, you're left feeling out of place.

These scenarios highlight why inclusivity in event planning is so crucial. When event organizers and HR professionals take the time to recognize and address the needs of all their attendees, including non-drinkers, they create spaces that are truly welcoming. This approach doesn't just improve the experience for non-drinkers—it enhances the event for everyone, fostering an environment where all attendees can connect, engage, and leave with a positive impression.

But even with the best intentions, things can go wrong if the execution isn't done thoughtfully. Let me share a recent experience that underscores the importance of detailed planning and proper training. At a conference where we were supporting their first attempt at offering non-alcoholic drink options, the organizers were eager to promote inclusivity. They decided to feature a special alcohol-free drink at their event, and to further emphasize this, they asked if we could provide our Sober Life Rocks mocktail stir sticks, emblazoned with our puzzle piece logo, to clearly mark the non-alcoholic beverages.

I was excited to see how this would play out and looked forward to spotting our logo in a few drinks here and there during the event. However, as the happy hour on the exhibit hall floor kicked off, I began to notice something odd—our stir sticks were showing up in nearly every drink, not just the alcohol-free ones.

Curious, I approached one of the attendees who was holding a drink with our stir stick and asked if her drink was alcohol-free. She responded that she had specifically requested a non-alcoholic beverage, and the bartender had assured her that it was. This struck me as strange, given how many drinks I was seeing with our stir sticks. I decided to investigate further and approached the bartender, who didn't know who I was.

I asked him about the stir sticks and which drink he was placing them into. He confidently told me he was using them in the "special" drink of the evening, a Hurricane, which they were featuring in honor of our New Orleans location. My heart sank because I knew that the Hurricane is traditionally a very potent alcoholic drink, and there was no alcohol-free version on the menu that I was aware of.

Concerned, I immediately checked in with the meeting planner, who quickly realized the mistake. The bartenders had not been properly informed and were inadvertently marking alcoholic drinks with the stir sticks meant only for non-alcoholic beverages. The planner swiftly corrected the situation, educating the bartenders that the only truly alcohol-free option was a simple orange juice-based drink.

Later, the same attendee I had spoken with earlier came up to me, laughing nervously. She said that after finishing her drink, she started to feel a bit giggly and soon found out it had alcohol in it after all. While she managed to laugh it off, I couldn't help but think about the potential consequences if she had been in recovery, counting her sober days, or early in a pregnancy. That could have been disastrous, not just socially, but personally and emotionally for her.

This experience underscores a critical lesson: no matter how well you plan an inclusive event, it's essential that every person involved in the execution understands the importance of their role. Whether it's the meeting planners, bartenders, or servers, everyone needs to be fully informed and trained to ensure that the event lives up to its inclusive ideals. It's these details that can make or break the experience for attendees, and in this case, it was a stark reminder that good intentions need to be backed by precise execution.

From an HR perspective, this responsibility takes on even greater significance when you are the host of the meeting or event. The last thing you want is an incident at your event that could have been prevented with better training or preparation. An inclusive environment isn't just about making everyone feel welcome—it's also about ensuring the safety and well-being of all participants. When alcohol is involved, the stakes are even higher. A misstep in service or a lack of understanding from staff can lead to uncomfortable situations, or worse, incidents that could reflect poorly on your organization and lead to potential liabilities.

As you'll see throughout this book, embracing sober-friendly practices is not just about responding to a trend—it's about setting a new standard for what professional gatherings should be. By doing so, you'll not only attract a broader audience but also ensure that your events are remembered for all the right reasons, while also protecting the reputation and integrity of your organization.

Chapter 2

MORE THAN A DRINK
The Lasting Benefits of Sober-Inclusive Conferences

The concept of sober inclusivity in event planning is gaining traction, reflecting a broader cultural shift towards mindful drinking and wellness. While this approach is still emerging, the benefits of hosting sober-inclusive events are multifaceted, positively impacting not just individual attendees but also the overall dynamics and reputation of the event and the organization hosting it.

There are more benefits to making an event more inclusive; here are just a few:

Enhanced Networking & Engagement: When the focus shifts away from standing just at the bar to order drinks, attendees are more likely to engage in genuine conversations and build professional connections based on shared interests rather than on the social rituals surrounding drinking. This change is particularly relevant today, as societal trends indicate a decrease in alcohol consumption and a growing interest in well-being and mindful living. Major alcohol and restaurant brands are responding to this shift by investing in non-alcoholic products, highlighting the market's recognition of changing consumer preferences. With guests more present and engaged throughout the event, the quality of interactions is enhanced, leading to more productive and lasting professional connections.

Positive Attendee Testimonials: Attendees of sober-inclusive events often report a more positive experience compared to traditional alcohol-centric gatherings. Many guests express appreciation for the availability of high-quality non-alcoholic options, which allow them to feel included and respected in their choices. This level of inclusivity contributes to a more enjoyable experience for all attendees, not just those who abstain from alcohol. When everyone feels their preferences are acknowledged and catered to, the overall atmosphere of the event becomes more welcoming and inclusive.

Sober Life Rocks collaborated with a conference that fully embraced the concept of offering inclusive beverage options. They set up two bars: one served four signature cocktails with alcohol, reminiscent of those you'd find at a typical cocktail reception. The second bar offered the exact same drinks, but without alcohol. The response was overwhelmingly positive and far exceeded expectations.

Guests were thrilled with the mocktail offerings, and by the end of the night, the mocktail bar had actually served twice as many drinks as the bar with alcohol. In post-event surveys, attendees expressed deep appreciation for the availability of these non-alcoholic options. Even those who usually drank alcohol found themselves opting for a mocktail for their second drink, valuing the chance to enjoy a fun, flavorful beverage without the worry of feeling sluggish the next day.

Many non-drinkers shared how much they appreciated having drinks that not only tasted great but also looked festive and fun, complete with umbrellas and flowers—just like the "real" ones. For the first time, they felt truly included in the event, without the need to "fake" drinking or feel isolated by their choice not to consume alcohol. The availability of these thoughtful options created a more welcoming and pressure-free environment, allowing everyone to enjoy the event on their own terms.

Boosting Company Image & Attendee Loyalty: Hosting inclusive events also serves to enhance a company's image by demonstrating a commitment to diversity and wellness. By addressing the needs of all attendees, including those who prefer non-alcoholic options, companies send a clear message that they value and respect individual preferences and are attuned to current societal trends. This approach not only boosts the company's reputation but also fosters increased loyalty among attendees. Employees and guests are more likely to appreciate and remember events where they felt truly included and catered to, making them more inclined to return for future events.

The Impact of Thoughtful Planning: Consider the experience of one of our members, who found herself in a difficult situation due to a lack of thoughtful event planning. She was a few years into her recovery, and although none of her coworkers knew about her sobriety, her boss was aware. At a big annual sales conference, she was honored as one of the top salespeople of the year—a career highlight she was incredibly proud of. However, the evening took a turn when her boss decided to take the team out bar hopping to celebrate their successes. Despite her suggestion to opt for dinner instead, the group overruled her, and they spent the night moving from one bar to the next, with shots and drinks flowing freely.

As the night wore on, she found herself increasingly isolated, trying to avoid drinking without drawing attention to herself. Eventually, she ended up in a bar bathroom, hiding in a stall, crying on the phone to her husband, unsure of what to do. What should have been the best day of her career turned into one of her worst. When she returned to the office the following week, she voiced her concerns, using an analogy that has stuck with me: "If we had an employee in a wheelchair on the team, we wouldn't plan a marathon as a team-building event." This experience underscores the importance of being thoughtful about all aspects of event planning, including after-hours activities, to ensure that every team member feels included and supported.

Embracing Sober Inclusivity: Incorporating sober inclusivity into event planning offers significant benefits that align with current societal trends, enhance the quality of networking, improve overall attendee satisfaction, and positively impact a company's image and reputation. As the sober-curious movement continues to grow, adopting these practices can set your events apart, ensuring they are successful and reflective of modern values.

From an HR perspective, these considerations are not just about inclusivity—they're about risk management and fostering a safe, respectful environment for all employees. By proactively addressing the needs of a diverse workforce, HR professionals can help prevent incidents that might arise from a lack of appropriate accommodations. This foresight not only protects the organization from potential liabilities but also promotes a culture of care and responsibility.

Legal Protections and the Need for Inclusive Event Planning: When planning professional events, it's crucial to recognize that inclusivity isn't just about creating a welcoming atmosphere—it's also about adhering to legal protections under the Americans with Disabilities Act (ADA). Individuals in recovery from addiction are protected under the ADA, which means that event planners, HR professionals, and venues must take into account the unique needs of these attendees. This includes ensuring that events do not pressure individuals to consume alcohol, providing adequate alcohol-free options, and training staff to be sensitive to the diverse needs of all participants. By doing so, you not only create a more inclusive environment but also mitigate potential legal risks and ensure compliance with federal regulations.

Understanding these legal obligations is vital for creating events that are truly inclusive. It highlights the responsibility of event planners and HR professionals to go beyond merely following trends and actively consider the legal and ethical implications of their event planning choices. Recognizing the protections offered by the ADA underscores the importance of thoughtful, inclusive event design that respects the rights and needs of all attendees, especially those in recovery.

Inclusivity in event planning goes far beyond simply meeting the basic needs of attendees. It's about creating an environment where every participant feels valued, respected, and fully engaged. When individuals feel genuinely included, they are more likely to participate fully and contribute positively to the event's overall atmosphere. This sense of belonging is crucial—it enhances attendees' psychological well-being, making them feel acknowledged and appreciated.

Understanding the psychological impact of inclusivity is essential for meeting planners and HR professionals alike. Crafting events that cater to a diverse range of preferences—whether related to dietary choices, social interactions, or sensory needs—sends a powerful message: each attendee's comfort and choices matter. When participants don't feel pressured to conform to any norm, they can interact more authentically and form more meaningful connections. This not only enhances individual experiences but also elevates the collective atmosphere, fostering a more welcoming and inclusive environment for everyone involved.

To achieve this, planners must thoughtfully consider every aspect of the event—from layout and activities to the variety of options available. By incorporating these insights into your event planning, you can transform how attendees perceive and experience your events, making them more inclusive, engaging, and ultimately, more successful. For HR professionals, this means contributing to a work culture where every employee feels respected, valued, and motivated to participate fully, thereby supporting the overall success of both the event and the organization.

"Embracing the idea of an alcohol free options at our conference was a game-changer, thanks to Laura's guidance.

The response from people that would have never been open to coming was overwhelmingly positive, with many expressing their appreciation for this inclusive option.

It not only added a unique and fun element to our event but also made everyone feel more welcome. I personally had people say this is why I did not come to the event in the past. Now I am going to give it a try!"

My best,
Elijah Desmond
Founder, The Dental Festival and Smiles at Sea
elijahdesmond.com

Chapter 3

IDENTIFYING YOUR AUDIENCE
Why You Have Not Recognized This Audience Before

When planning events, it's easy to overlook certain segments of your audience—especially those who are less visible or vocal about their needs. One such group that has been historically underrepresented in event planning is those who choose not to drink alcohol. Whether they are in recovery, abstain for health or personal reasons, or simply prefer not to drink, these individuals often navigate professional events in a way that keeps them under the radar, making it challenging for event planners to fully understand and meet their needs.

The Invisible Attendees: Why You Haven't Seen Them

The reality is, the sober audience at your events might be larger than you think, but they often go unnoticed. This is largely because many individuals who don't drink, or who drink sparingly, tend to keep a low profile. Let's explore why this is the case and how it affects their experience at your events:

Fitting In by Fading Out: Many sober attendees adopt strategies to blend in with the crowd, such as ordering a soda with a lime or a tonic water that looks like a cocktail, just to avoid questions or scrutiny. They don't want to stand out or seem different, so they quietly go along with the flow, participating in a way that doesn't draw attention to their choice not to drink. This desire to "fit in" can lead them to engage in behaviors that make them uncomfortable, or worse, cause them to leave events early to avoid the social pressure altogether.

Quiet Exits: Often, those who don't drink will quietly slip away once the event transitions into a more alcohol-focused phase, such as during after-hours networking events. Their departure is usually unnoticed because it happens discreetly. They might leave to avoid the awkwardness of their perception of being the only one not drinking, or because they simply don't enjoy being in an environment where the focus is on alcohol. As a result, they miss out on key networking opportunities, which is often a primary reason they attended the event in the first place.

Avoiding the Event Altogether: For some, the idea of attending a conference where much of the networking revolves around alcohol is enough to deter them from coming at all. They weigh the costs—both financial and personal—of attending an event that doesn't cater to their preferences or needs and often decide it's not worth it. These are potential attendees who might have been eager to participate, learn, and network, but choose not to because they don't see themselves fitting into the traditional event model.

Pressure to Conform: It's not just those who identify as sober who are affected by the alcohol-centric culture at many events. A significant portion of attendees who do drink might still prefer to moderate their intake but feel pressured to keep up with the social norms of the event. This pressure can lead them to drink more than they intended, simply because they don't want to stand out or because they feel that drinking is expected of them. While the decision to drink ultimately lies with the individual, the environment created by the event plays a significant role in influencing these choices.

A Professional Setting Gone Awry: A Personal Experience

To illustrate the impact of an alcohol-centric environment on attendees, let me share a personal experience from a conference I attended last year. During the day, the event was the epitome of professionalism. I observed numerous professionals engaging in meaningful meetings and conversations, with many young attendees striving to build better networks and advance their careers. The atmosphere was one of focus and ambition, with impeccably dressed individuals discussing business strategies and forging valuable connections.

However, the scene took a dramatic turn once the day transitioned into the evening. As the bars rolled out in the exhibit hall, shots were being poured, and heavy drinking was in full swing. The professionalism that had characterized the daytime dissipated on the dance floor, where inappropriate behavior and off-the-cuff remarks became commonplace. I found myself uncomfortable and typically would have retreated to my room, but the entertainment that evening featured Belinda Carlisle (from the Go-Go's—a nod to my 80s nostalgia), which kept me from leaving immediately.

As the night progressed, the stark contrast between the day and evening became more apparent. The once-respectable gathering descended into chaos, with the jovial atmosphere overshadowed by excessive drinking. Witnessing this shift was disheartening, especially considering the potential negative impact on attendees who prefer or need to remain sober. Some colleagues and I decided not to return to this conference the following year, choosing instead to support events that better respected diverse attendee needs. These individuals never voiced their reasons for skipping, and many event planners remain unaware of why attendees quietly choose not to return.

This year, the same conference took a different, yet equally problematic approach. On the second day, the leadership team took to the stage to discuss their own experiences with excessive drinking the night before, openly sharing how it left them feeling unwell the next day. While transparency is generally commendable, in this context, it served to glamorize a negative experience associated with alcohol consumption. Instead of promoting a balanced and inclusive environment, the conference inadvertently reinforced the notion that heavy drinking is a norm, further alienating those who do not wish to partake.

The Untapped Potential

Recognizing and catering to your sober or sober-curious audience is not just about inclusivity; it's about tapping into an untapped potential that could elevate the success of your events. When you create an environment where all attendees feel valued and comfortable, you foster a sense of belonging that enhances the overall experience for everyone involved.

Your event doesn't have to lose its vibrancy or excitement by reducing the focus on alcohol. Instead, it can gain a reputation as a place where connections are meaningful, interactions are genuine, and everyone—regardless of their drinking habits—feels like they belong.

As you move forward in planning your events, consider how you can bring these hidden audiences into the spotlight. Create spaces where they feel seen, respected, and fully able to participate. By doing so, you're not just filling a gap—you're setting a new standard for what it means to host a truly inclusive and successful event.

Chapter 4

RAISING THE BAR

The Crucial Role of Bars and Bartenders in Shaping Event Atmosphere

At far too many events, the black bar setup follows a predictable pattern: beer bottles lined up on one side, wine glasses on the other, and a small selection of sodas or bottled water tucked away in a corner for those who don't drink. When a full bar is offered, the options for non-drinkers barely improve, often limited to club soda with a lime or perhaps a tonic water. To make matters worse, these non-alcoholic drinks are sometimes served in different glasses, subtly signaling that those who choose not to drink are not quite equal in the eyes of the event.

This kind of setup does more than just limit options—it sends a message that the event prioritizes alcohol, and those who abstain are an afterthought. It creates a divide between those who drink and those who don't, often making the latter group feel less valued, less included, and even less welcome. The atmosphere of an event is significantly influenced by its bar and how drinks are presented, making it essential to rethink how we approach this integral part of the experience.

At first glance, the little things might seem insignificant, but in the world of event planning, it's often these small touches that can make the biggest difference. Let me share a few stories that illustrate how the thoughtful—or thoughtless—choices made by event organizers can profoundly impact the experience of attendees, particularly those who choose not to drink.

A Champagne Flute Without Consideration

I attended an elegant evening affair that seemed perfect in every way. The chandeliers cast a warm glow, and the room buzzed with laughter and conversation as waiters glided through the crowd, offering trays of champagne flutes. It was a picture-perfect scene—except for me (and I found out after, quite a few others in attendance) As I approached the entrance, a waiter extended a glass of bubbly my way. I politely declined, saying, "No thank you," but he insisted, almost pressing the glass into my hand. Suddenly, I found myself holding a champagne flute, feeling uncomfortable and out of place in a society that so often celebrates drinking as the norm.

When I asked if they had any non-alcoholic alternatives, I was met with a disappointing response: there were none. Later in the evening, I spoke with the meeting planner and shared my experience. She listened thoughtfully and, to her credit, reflected on the oversight. "You know," she said, "we really should have had sparkling juice or something similar in champagne glasses to ensure everyone feels included." It was a small, yet significant realization—one that underscored the importance of thoughtful event planning. Even in the most elegant settings, a little extra consideration can go a long way in making everyone feel welcome.

A Thoughtful Gesture: The Power of an Umbrella

In contrast, another event I attended highlighted how even the simplest acts of kindness can create a sense of inclusion. A fellow attendee, who herself enjoyed an alcohol infused margarita, took the initiative to ensure I felt just as included as everyone else. When margaritas were being handed out freely, she informed the waitress that I don't want one with alcohol and asked that the same waitress to bring my beverages directly to me, ensuring there was no confusion about my preferences. To make it even clearer, she requested that a different colored umbrella be placed in my mocktail—an orange one, to distinguish it from the alcoholic drinks.

This thoughtful gesture might seem small, but it had a profound impact on me. It not only made me feel welcome but also eliminated any potential for awkwardness or confusion. It was a simple act, but it demonstrated how much she cared about making sure everyone felt included, regardless of their drink choice.

A Clever Twist: Lemon Drops and the Power of Detail

Another memorable experience involved a creative bartender at an event who went out of his way to ensure both drinkers and non-drinkers were accommodated in a subtle, yet effective manner. The signature drink of the evening was a lemon drop, but with a clever twist: the alcoholic versions were garnished with lemons, while the non-alcoholic ones sported oranges. As drinks were passed around the table, it became immediately obvious which ones contained alcohol.

These stories serve as powerful reminders that the success of an event isn't just about the big, sweeping gestures, but also about the small, thoughtful details. By paying attention to these little things, event planners can create environments that make everyone feel valued, respected, and included. It's these seemingly minor considerations that ultimately make the difference between an event that is merely attended and one that is truly remembered.

When planning inclusive events, offering a selection of non-alcoholic beverages is just the beginning. The real impact lies in presenting these options as integral parts of the event, not merely as afterthoughts. By providing sophisticated, adult-friendly non-alcoholic beverages, you can significantly enhance the inclusivity of your event. These options aren't just for those who abstain from alcohol; they appeal to anyone who may wish to moderate their consumption throughout the event.

There are also important considerations regarding the setup of the bar area. A mixed bar—where alcoholic and non-alcoholic drinks are served side by side—can help ensure that those who don't drink don't feel singled out by having to visit a separate bar. This integrated approach fosters a sense of equality and inclusion, allowing everyone to enjoy their drinks without feeling different.

However, there are also distinct advantages to separating the bars. For one, it reduces the risk of accidentally serving alcohol to someone who has chosen not to drink. When non-alcoholic beverages are served at a dedicated bar, it's clear to both the server and the attendee what's being offered, minimizing the chances of a mix-up.

Another consideration is the method of serving drinks. Having a bartender mix drinks on the spot can be an inclusive experience for all involved, as many cocktails can easily be made without alcohol. This allows non-drinkers to feel just as much a part of the event as those who are consuming alcohol. On the other hand, offering non-alcoholic drinks that come in bottles or cans and are poured in front of the attendee provides an added layer of security—there's no chance of alcohol being included by mistake, as the attendee can see exactly what they're getting.

Balancing these options—integrating bars versus separating them, mixing drinks on the spot versus serving from bottles or cans—is key to creating an event that feels welcoming and inclusive for all attendees. Meeting planners must thoughtfully address these logistical challenges to ensure a successful and comfortable experience for everyone involved. By doing so, you not only support inclusivity but also create an environment that encourages meaningful engagement and connection among all participants.

Balancing Beverage Options: Alcoholic & Non-Alcoholic Selections

One of the key logistical challenges in event planning is achieving a balanced mix of alcoholic and non-alcoholic beverages. This balance is essential for catering to the diverse preferences of attendees and fostering an inclusive atmosphere where everyone feels valued and respected. Here are some strategies to effectively balance these options:

Better Representation: Non-alcoholic options should be just as varied and appealing as their alcoholic counterparts. This means offering mocktails, non-alcoholic wines, beers, or creatively crafted soft drinks. By providing more enticing choices, you ensure that every guest feels considered and included, regardless of their drinking preferences.

Visibility and Accessibility: It's important that non-alcoholic options are prominently displayed and easily accessible, just like alcoholic beverages. Consider setting up separate stations or even a dedicated non-alcoholic bar to highlight these options. This approach sends a clear message that non-alcoholic drinks are a valued part of the event's offerings, not just an afterthought.

Offering a selection of non-alcoholic beverages is crucial, but true inclusivity comes from integrating these options seamlessly into the event. Non-alcoholic drinks aren't just for those who abstain entirely; they also appeal to attendees who want to moderate their intake. It's important to consider that some people find the term "mocktails" off-putting, so using alternatives like "zero proof," "alcohol-free" (AF), or "NA" (non-alcoholic) can create a more welcoming atmosphere. However, be mindful that "NA" typically refers to drinks with trace amounts of alcohol, while "AF" guarantees no alcohol content at all.

There are benefits to mixing alcoholic and non-alcoholic options at the same bar, as it avoids singling out non-drinkers and makes everyone feel included. However, separate bars for alcoholic and alcohol-free drinks can reduce the risk of accidentally serving alcohol to those who don't want it. Offering drinks made on the spot, with or without alcohol, further enhances inclusivity, while serving from clearly labeled bottles or cans ensures guests know exactly what they're getting.

Drink Presentation: The presentation of non-alcoholic beverages should be just as creative and engaging as that of alcoholic drinks. Unique glassware, garnishes, and imaginative names for mocktails can elevate the experience, making these drinks attractive to all attendees, whether they usually consume alcohol or not.

Ultimately, the key is to provide a variety of appealing, well-branded non-alcoholic options that are as accessible and attractive as alcoholic ones, helping all attendees feel equally valued and included in the event.

Here's how you can enhance their appeal:

✦ **Flavor Complexity:** The most appealing mocktails are those that offer a sophisticated and complex flavor profile, akin to traditional cocktails. This can be achieved through the use of fresh ingredients, herbs, spices, and unique flavor combinations. To add depth and uniqueness, consider incorporating exotic fruits, longer herb infusions, or homemade syrups.

♦ **Presentation and Aesthetics:** The visual appeal of mocktails plays a crucial role in their success. Using attractive glassware, vibrant garnishes, and visually striking colors can make mocktails just as exciting as their alcoholic counterparts. Techniques like layering drinks, adding edible flowers, or using dry ice for dramatic effects can further enhance their presentation.

♦ **Healthier Options:** Many attendees are drawn to mocktails as a healthier alternative to alcoholic beverages. By using natural sweeteners, fresh juices, and avoiding artificial additives, you can increase their appeal. Offering low-sugar or sugar-free versions, incorporating superfoods, or using organic ingredients can attract health-conscious guests.

♦ **Inclusivity and Variety:** Mocktails cater to individuals who don't consume alcohol for various reasons, including health, religious beliefs, or personal preferences. Offering a wide variety of mocktails ensures there's something for everyone, further enhancing the inclusivity of your event. Expanding the menu to include a range of tastes—from sweet and fruity to bitter and herbaceous—can make these options even more inviting.

Recognizing that the full range of options available at a bar or restaurant may not be feasible at a roll-up bar during an event, it's still possible to offer sophisticated and refreshing alcohol-free beverages that go beyond the typical sweet mocktails of the past. While a restaurant or bar can create elaborate AF drinks using alternatives to liquor, event setups often lack the space and resources for such complexity. However, with a few standard bar ingredients, you can still craft enjoyable and refined drinks that cater to all attendees:

Cucumber Cooler

- **Ingredients:** Fresh cucumber slices, lime juice, soda water, a splash of simple syrup
- **Instructions:** Muddle cucumber slices with lime juice and simple syrup. Add ice, top with soda water, and garnish with a cucumber slice or mint.

Ginger Lime Fizz

- × **Ingredients:** Ginger beer, fresh lime juice, soda water

- × **Instructions:** Pour ginger beer and lime juice over ice, top with soda water, and garnish with a lime wedge.

Citrus Spritz

- **Ingredients:** Fresh orange juice, lemon juice, soda water
- **Instructions:** Mix orange juice and lemon juice over ice, top with soda water, and garnish with an orange or lemon slice.

Mint Lemonade

- **Ingredients:** Fresh lemon juice, mint leaves, simple syrup, water or soda water
- **Instructions:** Muddle mint leaves with simple syrup, add lemon juice, and top with water or soda water. Serve over ice with a mint sprig garnish.

Berry Smash

- **Ingredients:** Mixed berries (strawberries, raspberries, etc.), lime juice, simple syrup, soda water
- **Instructions:** Muddle berries with lime juice and simple syrup, add ice, top with soda water, and garnish with a few whole berries or a lime wedge.

Tropical Splash

- × **Ingredients:** Pineapple juice, coconut water, a splash of lime juice
- × **Instructions:** Shake all ingredients with ice, strain into a glass over fresh ice, and garnish with a pineapple slice or a cherry.

Virgin Mojito

- **Ingredients:** Fresh mint leaves, lime juice, sugar, soda water
- **Instructions:** Muddle mint leaves with lime juice and sugar, add ice, top with soda water, and garnish with a mint sprig and lime wedge.

Cranberry Spritzer

- **Ingredients:** Cranberry juice, soda water, a splash of lime juice
- **Instructions:** Mix cranberry juice and lime juice over ice, top with soda water, and garnish with a lime wedge.

These drinks provide a refreshing, sophisticated experience without alcohol, ensuring that all guests can enjoy a well-crafted beverage, even within the limitations of a more simplified event setup.

Adding a creative twist to the names of your alcohol-free drinks can elevate the experience for your attendees, making the beverages feel just as special as their alcoholic counterparts. You can even have fun by naming them after the conference, your business, or inside jokes that only your attendees might appreciate. For example, instead of a "Cucumber Cooler," you could call it the "Zen Garden Fizz" or something related to your event theme, like the "Conference Cooler." A "Mint Lemonade" could be reimagined as the "Mellow Mint Breeze" or the "CEO's Choice." For a more personalized touch, consider names like the "Team Spirit Spritz" or the "Networker's Nectar." These playful and themed names not only add flair but also create a memorable and engaging experience, helping to foster a sense of community and fun among your attendees.

Making It Easy and Obvious: One of the most significant ways to support inclusivity at your event is to make ordering non-alcoholic drinks as easy and straightforward as possible. Consider placing clear signage with drink options or displaying bottles alongside their alcoholic counterparts. For someone who doesn't drink, ordering in an environment where alcohol is prevalent can be intimidating. By making it easy for them to point to or quickly decide on a drink, you help them feel more comfortable and less self-conscious, allowing them to focus on enjoying the event rather than navigating the complexities of the bar.

Incorporating these strategies not only ensures a balanced offering of beverages but also creates a more welcoming environment for all attendees. Whether your guests are choosing non-alcoholic options for health, personal, or religious reasons, these thoughtful touches can significantly enhance their experience, making your event memorable for all the right reasons.

Bartender Awareness and Training: Raising the Bar on Inclusivity

Selecting the right drink offerings is only the first step in creating an inclusive event. Equally important is ensuring that the venue staff, particularly bartenders, are fully trained and prepared to meet the diverse needs of your attendees. Bartenders should not only know how to make a variety of alcoholic and non-alcoholic drinks but also understand the importance of presentation and inclusivity in their service.

Understanding the financial implications of beverage choices is also crucial for creating a successful and inclusive event. Venues often measure success through Per Cap Revenue—the total revenue divided by the number of guests. Typically, non-drinkers contribute minimally to this metric, often opting for water or soda. However, by introducing high-quality, premium-priced non-alcoholic beverages, venues can significantly increase Per Caps, turning non-drinkers into valuable contributors to the event's revenue stream.

F&B budgets are usually managed by focusing on maintaining a certain Cost of Goods Sold (COGS) percentage, often around 20%. Mocktails and other non-alcoholic beverages present a unique opportunity for venues to use cheaper ingredients to craft sophisticated, alcohol-free drinks that are perceived as high-value. This allows venues to charge cocktail-level prices while keeping COGS in check. Additionally, most venue contracts with distributors already include a range of non-alcoholic options, so offering these alternatives doesn't have to break any existing contracts. Event planners should encourage venues to explore what's available and make these options part of their regular offerings.

However, it's not just about the financials or the availability of options; it's about ensuring that the bartenders are trained to serve these beverages appropriately. For instance, at a recent conference, I experienced firsthand the challenges of creating a sober-inclusive environment. When I approached the bar to inquire about non-alcoholic options, the bartender, fatigued and struggling to hear me over the noise, responded dismissively. This kind of attitude can be incredibly disheartening for someone in recovery or simply trying to avoid alcohol, exacerbating feelings of anxiety and isolation.

To ensure that your chosen venue supports an inclusive environment, it's crucial to work with venue management to implement comprehensive staff training programs that include:

Awareness and Sensitivity Training: Educate venue staff on the importance of respecting guests' choices regarding alcohol consumption. This involves understanding the diverse reasons someone might choose not to drink—ranging from personal health to religious beliefs or recovery from addiction—ensuring that all staff members approach their roles with empathy and consideration.

Attention to Detail: Train venue staff to meticulously prepare and serve drinks according to the guest's request. This includes double-checking orders, especially when preparing mocktails or non-alcoholic beverages, to ensure no alcohol is inadvertently added. This attention to detail demonstrates a commitment to the safety and comfort of all attendees.

Communication Skills: Train staff to communicate effectively and discreetly with guests about their drink preferences. Instead of asking "Would you like a cocktail?" or "Do you prefer white or red wine?", staff should be comfortable asking more inclusive questions like "What can I get for you?" or suggesting non-alcoholic options without making assumptions.

Rapid Response Strategy: Equip venue staff with a clear protocol for addressing mistakes, such as accidentally serving an alcoholic drink to a non-drinker. Immediate, appropriate actions to correct the situation and ensure the guest's comfort and safety are crucial for maintaining trust and confidence among attendees.

For HR professionals, ensuring that these measures are in place is not just about creating a welcoming environment—

it's about mitigating risks and protecting the company. When bringing employees to an event, knowing that the venue staff is trained to handle diverse needs and situations lowers the risk of incidents, such as an inappropriate service or a situation that could lead to discomfort or even harm. This level of preparation contributes to a safer, more inclusive environment, reducing the likelihood of any issues that could reflect poorly on the company or create liability concerns.

By ensuring that the venue staff is well-trained and prepared, event planners and HR professionals can create an environment where every guest feels respected and valued. A well-prepared team, combined with thoughtful drink offerings, can significantly enhance the inclusivity of the event, ensuring that all attendees feel comfortable and supported from the moment they arrive. This level of preparedness is key to making your event not just successful, but memorable for all the right reasons.

Chapter 5

STRATEGIC PARTNERSHIPS
Planning a Sober-Friendly Event with Venue Collaboration and Alcohol-Free Brand Integration

Planning a sober-friendly event is an essential step towards creating a more inclusive environment at conferences, but it requires careful consideration and strategic partnerships, particularly when it comes to working with venues. While the demand for alcohol-free options is growing, the reality is that many meeting and conference venues are still catching up with the trend. This chapter will guide you through the necessary negotiations and strategies to successfully collaborate with venues and integrate alcohol-free brands into your event.

Understanding the Venue Landscape: One of the first challenges you'll encounter when planning a sober-friendly event is the resistance or hesitation from venues, particularly in the food and beverage (F&B) departments. These departments often operate under longstanding contracts with alcohol suppliers and may not have prioritized alcohol-free options in the past. This can be due to several reasons, and it is important to spell them out here so you are prepared to know what you might be up against.

Lack of Awareness: Unlike restaurants and bars, which have begun to incorporate alcohol-free options into their menus, many conference centers and hotels have been slower to adapt. This is often because the demand from conference organizers has not been as vocal or consistent.

Contractual Obligations: F&B departments may cite existing contracts with alcohol suppliers as a reason for not offering a wider range of alcohol-free beverages. However, these contracts often do not cover non-alcoholic options, providing an opportunity for you to introduce these choices.

Budget Concerns: Venues might be concerned that incorporating alcohol-free options could strain their budgets. However, this is largely a misconception, as alcohol-free options are generally less expensive than their alcoholic counterparts.

Negotiating with Venues

To successfully introduce alcohol-free options into your event, it's crucial to approach venue negotiations with a clear strategy.

Be Persistent and Informed: As the event organizer, you are the client, and you have the right to request what you need for your attendees. Approach negotiations with a solid understanding of the sober movement and the benefits of offering alcohol-free options. Present your case with confidence, emphasizing the growing demand for inclusivity at events.

Leverage the Lack of Alcohol-Free Contracts: If the venue currently lacks a contract for alcohol-free beverages, this is an opportunity for flexibility. Since many venues do not have restrictions on what non-alcoholic options they can offer, you have the freedom to introduce new and innovative brands. Use this leverage to push for the inclusion of alcohol-free options that align with your event's inclusive goals.

Highlight Cost Benefits: Remind the venue that alcohol-free options are generally more cost-effective than alcoholic beverages. By offering these alternatives, they can potentially reduce their overall beverage costs while enhancing the event's appeal to a broader audience. This can be a compelling argument, especially if the venue is concerned about budget constraints.

Partner with Alcohol-Free Brands

Incorporating alcohol-free brands into your event not only enhances the attendee experience but also opens up valuable partnership opportunities. Many alcohol-free brands are eager to get their products into the hands of consumers, especially at high-visibility events. This might also be an option to present to the venues that can't bring in new companies on their own, but you can within your meeting or conference, as a sponsor or as part of your event.

Here's how you can leverage these partnerships:

Seek Out Brand Collaborations: Reach out to alcohol-free brands that align with the values of your event. (For a list of ones that would be eager to work with you, connect with Sober Life Rocks) These brands are often willing to provide their products at a discounted rate or even sponsor parts of your event in exchange for exposure. This can be a win-win situation, as it provides your attendees with high-quality options while also giving the brands a platform to reach new customers.

Introduce Brands to Venues: Many venues may not yet be familiar with the range of alcohol-free options available. By partnering with brands, you can help introduce these products to the venue, potentially paving the way for future events to offer these choices as well. This not only benefits your event but also contributes to a broader shift in the industry towards more inclusive offerings.

Here are a few that we are fans of!

ALCOHOL FREE & ZERO PROOF BRANDS

Uptime Brewing: IPA and Golden Lager
Contact: Troy Joos, Founder 512-200-4525

We believe it's time for a better beer. With a commitment to the highest quality ingredients, responsible sourcing, and minimizing our environmental footprint, we have crafted the first functional non-alcoholic beers brewed in the United States. Our beers are adaptogenic, low calorie, vegan friendly, a source of natural electrolytes, and free of any artificial flavors or preservatives. We're on a mission to enable people to enjoy themselves, their nights, and their mornings.

• •

MixoloSHE: 7 flavor varieties mimicking a cocktail
Contact: Benny Smeds, Co-Founder 347-326-4839

Bar-Quality Non-Alcoholic Cocktails in a Can: We make alcohol-free cocktails that are just as good as your regular ones. In fact, they are better, because no brain cell casualties here. Packed with all-natural flavors, we guarantee you're in for a tasty treat.

Curious Elixers: 7 flavor varieties (not meant to mimic a cocktail)
Contact: Rachel Reynolds,rachel@goodbusiness.works

We created Curious Elixirs because we believe non-alcoholic drinks should be unusually delicious, well-crafted, and good for bodies and souls. Our flavors are bold and crafted for the adventurous. Each flavor is a collaboration between our team of world-class bartenders, herbalists, and food scientists, and we proudly use only organic juices, herbs, spices, roots, barks, and botanicals to make your mouth dance. was used in Mayan culture as an aphrodisiac.

RSRV Collective: 4 flavor varieties (vaguely reminiscent of a cocktail)
Contact: Alec Senese, Founder, alec@rsrvcollective.com

RSRV Collective Kenshō Cocktails are expertly crafted to give you the experience of luxury and sophistication, without the negative side-effects of alcohol. RSRV Collective cocktails are vegan, gluten-free, non-GMO and contain no known allergens.

• •

MixoloSHE: Tequila, Whiskey and Gin
Contact: Benny Smeds, Founder 347-326-4839

The only non-alcoholic Spirit that isn't encouraging you to cover up its taste. Drink us neat, on the rocks, or use to make your favorite drink without the hangover.

Tenneyson: On the rocks alternative
Contact: Graham Wasilition, Founder graham@tenneyson.com

Tenneyson created the world's most bold, liquid botanical drink, for big thinkers, high performers, and those with outrageously good taste. Meant for those who used to have a drink on the rocks, this unique drink is strong enough to stand alone but dynamic enough to coexist in a no, or low proof cocktail. We don't mock the flavors or effects of traditional liquor categories like whiskey or gin. We do our own thing.

• •

Giesen: Sparking Brut, Sauvignon Blanc, Pinot Gris, Riesling, Rose, Merlot
Contact: Jeremy Snyder, US Brand Director, jeremy@giesengroup.co.nz

The New Zealand wines of Giesen win awards year after year, and these 0% alcohol wines are the same as their award-winning counterparts, just with the alcohol removed!

Drink Joyus: Sparking wine, Sparkling Rose, Cabernet Sauvignon, Rose
Contact: Mikayla Neves, Founder mikayla@drinkjoyus.com

Jøyus® is the first award winning non-alcoholic wine that tastes like wine, created by people that don't drink. We're not making fancy juice here people. This stuff tastes like the real thing, just with the alcohol removed. I created these delicious non-alcoholic wines so people everywhere could have an adult option that was as close to the real thing as possible. Our alcohol-removed wines taste, feel and look like real wine. So if you want to live life happy, joyous and alcohol-free, then Jøyus® is perfect for you.

In order to receive any specials the company might offer when ordering, mention referral from Sober Life Rocks

For more info email us at: info@soberliferocks.com

Create Lasting Impact: Remember that your event can set a precedent. If you successfully integrate alcohol-free options into the venue's offerings, you're not just enhancing your event—you're potentially influencing the venue's approach to future events. As more organizers begin to request these options, the venue will become more accustomed to providing them, ultimately making it easier for everyone to host inclusive events.

Once your conference is over, another event will take its place, and the venue will move on to its next client. However, the impact of your negotiations and partnerships can have lasting effects. By setting the standard for what a sober-friendly, inclusive event looks like, you're not just planning for the present—you're helping to shape the future of event planning.

The changes you implement today can influence how venues approach their offerings moving forward, making it easier for the next event planner to continue the trend towards inclusivity. This ripple effect can lead to a broader industry-wide shift, benefiting attendees and organizers alike.

Planning a sober-friendly event might require strategic partnerships and thoughtful negotiations, but you're not alone in this journey. By collaborating with venues and alcohol-free brands, you can create an event that meets the needs of all attendees and sets a new standard for inclusivity in the industry. Sober Life Rocks offers a range of resources to support you in this process, from downloadable checklists on our website to consultation services tailored to your specific needs. We also provide education options for your team, attendees, and venues. Plus, we can connect you with amazing AF brands that would be perfect for your event. With persistence, knowledge, and the right support, you can ensure that your event is not just another conference, but a pioneering step towards a more inclusive future.

Chapter 6

PLANNING THE PERFECT VENUE
Making Spaces that Support Inclusivity

Inclusivity also means addressing the environmental aspects of the venue. Noise levels, lighting, and even the layout of furniture can either enhance or detract from the inclusivity of an event. For instance, some attendees may find loud environments overwhelming, making quieter zones essential for fostering deeper connections. By carefully selecting and designing venues that accommodate a wide array of needs, planners can create spaces that are truly inclusive, ensuring that every attendee feels comfortable, respected, and able to participate fully.

Ultimately, the goal is to usher in a new era of event planning, one that is not merely reactive to trends but is deeply rooted in the recognition and respect for the diverse preferences of today's professionals. By curating inclusive, engaging, and comfortable environments, meeting planners are setting a new standard for professional events, ensuring their relevance and effectiveness in a landscape that values diversity and inclusivity above all.

Layout Considerations: Designing Spaces that Support Inclusivity

A thoughtfully designed layout can accommodate a diverse range of needs and preferences, ensuring that everyone feels welcome and able to engage fully. Below are some strategies and examples to help you create a layout that promotes inclusivity and enhances the attendee experience:

Creating an Inviting Atmosphere for Connection: The atmosphere of your event plays a crucial role in fostering inclusivity and ensuring everyone feels comfortable and engaged. One key factor in achieving this is controlling the ambient noise. A well-curated soundscape can enhance the atmosphere without drowning out conversations. If you're planning to have a DJ or live music, consider starting with a lower volume at the beginning of the event. This allows attendees to easily connect and converse, setting a relaxed tone as they arrive. As the evening progresses and people become more comfortable, the volume can gradually increase to encourage dancing and singing along.

Balancing the auditory elements with the visual can create an environment where attendees can both enjoy the festivities and engage in meaningful conversations, making the event memorable and inclusive for all.

Designated Networking-Friendly Zones: Create specific zones where attendees can take a break from the noise and intensity of the main event areas. These quieter spaces are ideal for networking in a more relaxed and intimate setting, particularly benefiting introverts or those who prefer one-on-one conversations. For example, set up a lounge area with comfortable seating, soft lighting, and plants to create a calming atmosphere. Ensure these zones are well-marked and easily accessible, ideally adjacent to more active areas so that attendees can transition smoothly between different environments.

Clear and Effective Signage: Navigation is crucial for ensuring attendees can move comfortably throughout the event space. Use clear, well-placed signage to guide attendees to different zones, restrooms, exits, and specific event areas. For example, color-coded signs with easily recognizable symbols can help attendees quickly locate where they need to go, whether it's the main stage, a quiet zone, or the buffet. Additionally, consider using digital displays that can be updated in real time to reflect any changes in the schedule or event layout.

Varied Seating Arrangements: Incorporate a range of seating options to cater to different preferences and physical needs. This might include traditional table-and-chair setups for formal discussions, comfortable lounge areas with sofas and armchairs for informal chats, and standing tables for those who prefer to move around or need a quick place to set down their drinks. For instance, placing standing tables near food stations encourages casual conversations while attendees grab a bite, while quieter lounge areas on the edges of the room offer a retreat from the hustle.

Ample Movement Space: Ensure there is enough space for attendees to move around comfortably without feeling crowded, especially in networking areas where groups may naturally form. Wide aisles, open spaces, and strategically placed seating can prevent bottlenecks and make it easier for people to circulate. For instance, avoid placing furniture too close to entrances or exits, which can create congestion, and instead, use open areas near the center of the room for spontaneous group gatherings.

Adaptable Spaces: Consider how your layout can adapt throughout the event. For instance, a space used for a keynote presentation might later transition into a networking area. Using modular furniture or movable walls can help you easily reconfigure the space as needed, ensuring that it continues to meet the needs of your attendees throughout the event.

My best example of this is when I spoke at a conference in a hotel in Idaho. After speaking all day in a traditional lecture style room set for about 200 people, I went back to my room to change and regroup for the evening event. Much to my surprise, when I walked into the very same room that I had spoken in all day, it had been completely transformed into a vibrant dueling piano bar. The rows of chairs and lecture-style setup were gone, replaced with round tables that invited conversation and mingling. Two low stages stood at opposite ends of the room, each with a grand piano ready for the evening's entertainment.

The atmosphere had shifted entirely—what was once a space for learning and discussion had become a lively and engaging social hub. The soft lighting and the lively banter of the piano players drew everyone in, creating an energy that was contagious. Attendees who had been focused and serious just hours before were now laughing, singing along, and even dancing.

The best part was that the transition was seamless. The room had adapted to the needs of the event, allowing the conference to flow naturally from professional development during the day to relaxed networking and fun in the evening. This thoughtful use of adaptable space not only enhanced the attendee experience but also ensured that everyone felt connected and engaged throughout the entire event.

By the end of the night, it was clear that the room's transformation had made a significant impact—people stayed late, fully immersed in the experience, and the sense of connection was palpable. It was a perfect example of how adaptable spaces can elevate an event, creating opportunities for engagement and enjoyment that last long after the formal sessions have ended.

Creating an inclusive environment at professional events involves much more than offering a variety of drink options; it requires thoughtful planning of every aspect of the event space. By considering these layout strategies, meeting planners can ensure their events are welcoming and engaging for all attendees, regardless of their preferences or needs.

Chapter 7

CREATIVE PROGRAMMING
Engaging Activities That Don't Eliminate Alcohol but Also Don't Revolve Around Alcohol

Creating an inclusive event is also about curating experiences that foster genuine connections among attendees. Thoughtful agenda and programming that engages all participants and creates memorable, meaningful interactions can transform your event into a success.

Here's how to design programming that doesn't just include everyone but makes them feel truly valued—without alcohol being the central focus.

Inclusive Activities: Engaging Everyone

The activities offered play a crucial role in fostering inclusivity. Dueling pianos is a great example of not only making the space inclusive, but also setting it up as an activity. Throughout the night there were people coaxing each other on stage to sing and dance. There were competitions with audience participation and when the lights came on at the end of the night, the room was still full of people and energy. I guarantee that by the amount of cell phone videos I saw being taken, not only did that group have a memorable time, they also created FOMO (fear of missing out) to those at home that did not make it but will next year.

Oh, did I mention that they had bars there too and lots of drinking but it was not the focal point of the night. Everyone at that event stayed and felt included.

Here are some creative ideas that keep the focus on engagement and interaction, rather than alcohol:

Group Games and Challenges: Incorporating activities that promote teamwork and interaction is a fantastic way to get attendees to connect and engage with each other. These activities can range from trivia quizzes and escape room challenges to collaborative puzzles that encourage participants to work together. The key is to choose games and challenges that are not only fun but also relevant to the event's theme, helping attendees' bond over shared experiences.

Here are a few examples I've seen or participated in that really stood out:

- **Scavenger Hunt Around the Hotel:** Organize a scavenger hunt that takes participants around the hotel or conference venue, with exciting prizes awaiting the winners at the end. This activity encourages teamwork and adds an element of adventure to the event.

- **80's Theme Night with Arcade Games:** Transform the venue into a nostalgic 80's arcade, complete with classic games like Pac-Man, pinball, and air hockey. An 80's cover band can provide live music, setting the perfect atmosphere for attendees to play and socialize.

- **Lounge Games:** Set up a relaxed area with games like giant Jenga, cornhole, card games, and more. These activities are perfect for facilitating conversations and helping attendees break the ice in a casual, enjoyable setting.

- **Speed Networking Sessions:** Implement a speed networking session, where participants have short, timed interactions with a series of other attendees. This is an efficient way for everyone to meet and make connections within a structured environment.

- **DIY Craft Stations:** Create DIY craft stations where attendees can engage in creative activities like making personalized name badges, decorating tote bags, or crafting small keepsakes. This hands-on approach fosters creativity and provides a unique way for participants to connect.

- **Charity Auction or Raffle:** Organize a charity auction or raffle during the event. Participants can bid on or win items donated by sponsors, with proceeds going to a charitable cause. This not only adds excitement but also promotes a sense of community and goodwill.

- **Fake Money Gambling Room:** Set up a fun, fake money gambling room with games like poker, blackjack, or roulette. Attendees can use "fun money" to bet and win prizes, creating a lively atmosphere without the pressure of real stakes.

Interactive Events: Engaging Attendees in Fun and Memorable Ways

Interactive events are a fantastic way to break down barriers and encourage attendees to get involved, creating lasting memories and building stronger connections. By incorporating activities that require participation, you make the event more engaging and inclusive for everyone. Here are some ideas for interactive events that can elevate your gathering:

- **Karaoke or Bar Trivia Games:** Set up a karaoke stage or host a bar trivia game where attendees can show off their singing talents or test their knowledge on various topics. These activities are great icebreakers and can turn strangers into friends through shared laughter and friendly competition.

- **Comedy Acts or Entertainment Shows with Audience Involvement:** Bring in a comedian or an entertainment act that involves the audience, such as improv or magic shows where participants are invited on stage. This kind of entertainment not only provides laughs but also creates a shared experience that everyone can enjoy and talk about afterward.

- **DJ or Band with a Diverse Playlist:** Hire a DJ or live band that plays a wide variety of music genres, ensuring that there's something for everyone to enjoy. From classic hits to current favorites, the key is to keep the dance floor lively and inclusive, appealing to all musical tastes.

- **Costume or Theme Parties:** Organize a costume or theme party where attendees are encouraged to dress up according to a specific theme. Whether it's a masquerade ball, a '70s disco night, or a tropical luau, theme parties allow guests to let loose and immerse themselves in the event, creating a vibrant and fun atmosphere.

- **Auction:** Host a live or silent auction where attendees can bid on a variety of items, from experiences to memorabilia. Not only does this add an element of excitement and competition, but it also serves as a fantastic way to raise money for a good cause. It's a win-

win that can bring everyone together for a common purpose while having fun.

These interactive events help make your gathering more dynamic and inclusive, ensuring that everyone has an opportunity to participate, connect, and create lasting memories.

Cultural or Local Experiences: Immersing Attendees in the Event's Surroundings

Enhance your event by incorporating cultural or local experiences that reflect the unique characteristics of your location or the diverse backgrounds of your attendees. These activities not only provide a deeper connection to the event's setting but also offer participants a chance to experience something new and memorable. Here are some ideas for integrating cultural or local elements into your event:

- **Local Cuisine Tasting:** Organize a food tasting that highlights the regional specialties of the event's location. For example, if your conference is in New Orleans, you could offer a tasting of local dishes like gumbo, jambalaya, and beignets. This not only provides a delicious experience but also introduces attendees to the culinary heritage of the area.

- **Cultural Performances:** Feature local musicians, dancers, or theater groups to showcase the cultural richness of the event's location. For example, a conference in Hawaii could include a traditional hula dance performance, while an event in Nashville might feature a live country music act. These performances add a unique local flavor to your event and allow attendees to experience the culture of the area firsthand.

- **Art Exhibits or Local Craft Fairs:** Collaborate with local artists to display their work or set up a craft fair where attendees can purchase handmade goods. For instance, in Santa Fe, you could host an exhibit of Native American art, or in Portland, feature a craft fair with local artisans showcasing their wares. This not only supports the local art scene but also provides attendees with the opportunity to take home a unique souvenir.

- **Historical or Cultural Tours:** Arrange guided tours that explore the history or culture of the event's location. In Washington, D.C., you could offer a tour of the city's iconic monuments and museums, or in San Francisco, a walking tour of historic neighborhoods like Chinatown or the Mission District. These tours give attendees a deeper understanding of the area and its significance.

- **Local Entertainment:** Hire performers or entertainment that is native to the area, such as a mariachi band in Texas, a jazz trio in New Orleans, or a bluegrass group in Kentucky. This local touch can make the evening more special and give attendees a genuine taste of the region's musical heritage.

These cultural and local experiences add depth and authenticity to your event, making it not just a gathering but a memorable exploration of the area's unique character.

Creating an inclusive event isn't just about providing options—it's about weaving those options into a cohesive, engaging experience that resonates with all attendees. Whether it's through carefully curated beverages, interactive activities, or thoughtful programming, the goal is to make every participant feel like they belong.

Chapter 8

MARKETING YOUR EVENT
Attracting Attendees to your Sober-Friendly event

Creating an inclusive and sober-friendly event is just the first step. The real challenge—and opportunity—lies in effectively marketing this unique experience to attract attendees who will appreciate and benefit from the thoughtful, inclusive meeting or conference. In a landscape where traditional conferences often focus on alcohol-centric networking, your event needs to stand out as a beacon of connection, wellness, and inclusivity. This chapter will guide you through the strategies to successfully market your sober-friendly event, ensuring that your audience understands it's about much more than just mocktails.

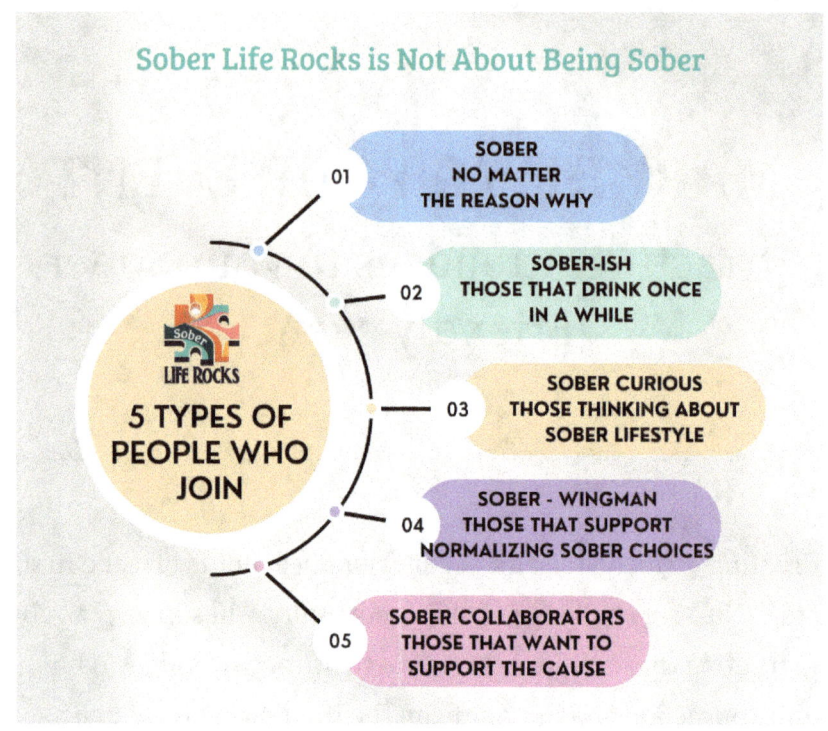

Market the Idea of Connection, Not Just a Replacement for Alcohol

When promoting the event, emphasize that the focus is on building meaningful connections rather than simply replacing alcohol with non-alcoholic options. Highlight how your event is designed to foster authentic relationships and deep networking opportunities in an inclusive environment. This approach will appeal not only to those who are sober or sober-curious but also to attendees who are tired of the standard conference fare of endless happy hours and superficial interactions.

For instance, your marketing materials could include messages like:

- 💬 *"Join us for an event where connections matter more than cocktails."*

- 💬 *"Experience networking reimagined—where the focus is on people, not drinks."*

- 💬 *"Connect deeply, network meaningfully, and leave feeling fulfilled."*

These types of messages shift the focus from what's being left out (alcohol) to what's being gained—genuine human connection.

Spotlight Inclusive Entertainment and Programming

Your event's programming and entertainment should be a key feature in your marketing efforts. Emphasize that your event offers diverse and engaging activities that don't revolve around alcohol but still offer plenty of fun and interaction. Whether it's live music, comedy acts, wellness lounges, or cultural performances, make sure these elements are front and center in your promotional materials.

By showcasing these aspects, you signal to potential attendees that your event is thoughtfully designed to include everyone, regardless of their preferences or lifestyle choices. Use taglines such as:

- 💬 *"Entertainment that connects, activities that inspire."*
- 💬 *"Inclusive events where everyone is welcome and every experience counts."*
- 💬 *"Crafting experiences that go beyond the ordinary, for everyone."*

These highlights will help create a perception of your event as dynamic, engaging, and different from the norm.

Leverage Influencers and Internal Champions

Identifying and collaborating with influencers or key figures within your industry who align with your event's inclusive mission can significantly amplify your marketing efforts. These individuals could be sober, sober-curious, or even "sober wingmen" who support others in their choice to abstain. Offer incentives for these influencers to promote your event—whether through social media posts, blog articles, or personal testimonials—highlighting the inclusive nature of your conference.

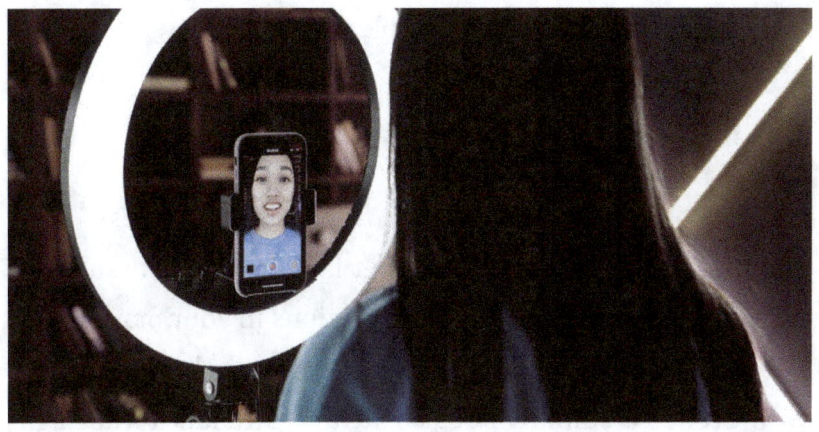

For example, you could provide free tickets, VIP access, or the opportunity to host a session at the event to encourage their participation. Their endorsement not only lends credibility to your event but also helps reach a broader audience, particularly those who might not have considered attending a sober-friendly conference before.

Carefully Curate Your Visual Imagery

The images you use in your marketing materials speak volumes about your event's atmosphere and priorities. Avoid featuring alcohol in any photos related to after-hours events or networking sessions. Instead, choose images that highlight diverse groups of people engaging in meaningful conversations, participating in interactive activities, or enjoying the inclusive entertainment you've planned.

Remember, visual storytelling is powerful—use it to show potential attendees that your event is a place where they can truly connect and feel comfortable.

Highlight Your Collaborations

If you're partnering with alcohol-free brands, wellness organizations, or groups like Sober Life Rocks, make sure to prominently feature these collaborations in your marketing efforts. Highlighting these partnerships not only enhances your event's credibility but also attracts attendees who align with the values of these organizations.

When promoting your agenda, particularly the aspects that typically focus on alcohol, such as evening receptions or networking dinners, make sure to mention your collaboration with these partners. This could include sponsored alcohol-free bars, wellness lounges, or specific sessions focused on mindful living. By doing so, you reinforce the message that your event is inclusive, forward-thinking, and committed to offering something unique and valuable.

Tailor The Messaging to Highlight Inclusivity

Throughout all your marketing channels—whether it's email campaigns, social media posts, or press releases—ensure that the messaging consistently highlights the inclusive nature of your event. Use language that welcomes everyone, regardless of what's in their cup, and positions your event as a space where all are valued and respected.

For example:

- *"At [Your Event], everyone is welcome—whether you're here for the connections, the content, or the community."*
- *"We believe in creating spaces where every attendee can thrive, connect, and contribute."*
- *"Join us for an event that celebrates diversity, wellness, and the power of genuine connections."*

These messages help to create a narrative around your event that is inviting, inclusive, and aligned with the values of a broad audience.

Engage with Your Audience Early and Often

Finally, remember that successful event marketing is an ongoing process. Start engaging with your potential attendees well before the event and maintain that connection through regular updates and interactive content. Use social media to create anticipation, share sneak peeks of the event's highlights, and build a community around your event long before it begins.

Host pre-event webinars or Q&A sessions with key speakers or influencers to give potential attendees a taste of what to expect. This not only builds excitement but also helps establish a rapport with your audience, making them more likely to attend and engage with your event.

Market with Purpose and Inclusivity

Marketing your sober-friendly event is about much more than just promoting the absence of alcohol; it's about showcasing the value of connection, inclusivity, and meaningful engagement. By carefully curating your messaging, visuals, and partnerships, and by leveraging the power of influencers and inclusive programming, you can attract a diverse and engaged audience.

Remember, your event has the potential to set a new standard in the industry, one that prioritizes the well-being and satisfaction of every attendee. Through thoughtful marketing, you can ensure that your event not only attracts attendees but also leaves a lasting impact—one that they'll remember long after the conference is over.

And as you take these steps to promote your event, consider partnering with Sober Life Rocks. We can offer a unique perspective and support to ensure that your event not only meets but exceeds the expectations of all your attendees. Together, we can create an environment that honors and celebrates every individual, ensuring that they leave your event feeling connected, fulfilled, and ready to take on the world.

Chapter 9

CREATING A WELCOMING ENVIRONMENT

Tips to Make It Easier for Attendees to Feel Included Before They Even Arrive

Inclusivity begins long before your attendees set foot in the venue. It starts with the efforts you make to ensure they feel welcomed, informed, and included from the moment they register. By thoughtfully planning pre-event engagement and setting the right tone, you can create an environment where everyone feels like they belong.

Pre-Event Engagement: Building Connections Early

Engaging attendees before the event helps to break the ice and foster a sense of community. There are many ways to achieve this, depending on your meeting size, attendees and budget.

Pre-Event Forums, Chat Groups, and Meet-and-Greet Sessions: Depending on the size of your meeting, you might choose to manage pre-event interactions yourself or use a specialized app to streamline the process. Start by establishing online forums or chat groups where attendees can begin engaging with each other, sharing their goals, and suggesting discussion topics. Hosting virtual meet-and-greet sessions is another effective strategy—these can be organized by industry, job role, or specific interests, helping participants find common ground and start building relationships before the event even begins.

For a more seamless experience, consider using apps like Whova, Brella, or Slack to facilitate these interactions. These platforms offer features like discussion boards, personalized agendas, and messaging capabilities, allowing attendees to connect based on shared interests and event goals. This early interaction not only helps attendees feel more connected from the start but also ensures that networking and discussions are more meaningful when everyone finally meets in person.

Communicate Well and Often: One of the keys to a successful event is effective communication with your attendees, starting well before the event date. Let them get excited about what's to come by sharing some of the special activities, speakers, and unique experiences you've planned. Regular updates can help build anticipation and engagement, ensuring that participants are looking forward to the event.

For many, attending a conference can be overwhelming, especially if they are unsure of what to expect. The more information you provide in advance, the more comfortable and welcomed attendees will feel upon arrival. Consider sending out detailed emails, newsletters, or using event apps to keep everyone informed about logistics, schedules, and highlights of the event. By keeping the lines of communication open and offering reassurance through these updates, you set the stage for a more inclusive and successful gathering.

Organize and Let Them Know of Scheduled Meet-Up Events: One of the most valuable aspects of any conference is the opportunity to connect with others—whether it's networking with peers, engaging with speakers, or finding like-minded individuals who share similar interests. To facilitate these connections, it's essential to organize and clearly communicate scheduled meet-up events throughout your conference.

These meet-ups can be tailored to various groups within your audience. For example, at Sober Life Rocks, we host specific meetups for our community members, providing a welcoming space where individuals who choose a sober lifestyle can connect and support one another. These types of gatherings can be incredibly empowering, offering attendees a sense of belonging and the chance to build meaningful relationships.

In addition to specialized meetups, consider offering broader opportunities for attendees to connect. You might organize sessions where participants can meet with industry peers they wouldn't ordinarily encounter, or host informal gatherings where attendees can chat with speakers and other thought leaders in a more relaxed setting. Other ideas could include themed meetups based on industry sectors, job roles, or even hobbies and interests.

By scheduling and promoting these meet-up opportunities, you encourage attendees to engage more deeply with the event and with each other. This not only enhances their overall experience but also fosters a sense of community that can extend far beyond the conference itself.

Ensuring your attendees feel welcomed and connected before they even step foot in the conference venue is key to creating a successful event. These pre-event strategies help attendees feel excited, informed, and at ease, paving the way for more meaningful interactions and a more vibrant conference atmosphere. By the time they arrive, they'll already feel like they're part of something special setting the stage for a truly memorable event.

Chapter 10

THE FUTURE OF EVENT PLANNING
Trends in Inclusivity and Sober Events

As the landscape of event planning continues to evolve, the future of successful event planning hinges on our ability to adapt and respond to the diverse needs of all attendees. Gathering and incorporating attendee feedback is not just a best practice—it's a crucial component in staying ahead of these trends and ensuring that events are more inclusive and effective with each iteration.

The Role of Feedback in Shaping Inclusive Events: In the context of the evolving event planning industry, feedback serves as a vital tool for understanding the effectiveness of inclusivity efforts and sober-friendly initiatives. It offers planners a window into the attendee experience, highlighting areas of success and those that require improvement. As events become more inclusive, it's essential to systematically gather and apply feedback to ensure that these efforts are meeting their goals and setting the stage for future innovations in event design.

Post-Event Surveys

A Comprehensive Tool for Continuous Improvement: Digital post-event surveys remain one of the most efficient ways to collect feedback on inclusivity. These surveys should be designed to capture a holistic view of the attendee experience, touching on everything from the accessibility of venues to the inclusivity of activities. A well-rounded survey might ask attendees to rate their satisfaction with the variety of programming, the effectiveness of sober-friendly options, and their overall sense of belonging. Open-ended questions like, "What could we have done to make the event more inclusive for you?" provide attendees with the opportunity to share specific insights that can guide future planning.

Real-Time Feedback Mechanisms

Adapting On the Fly: Real-time feedback will become increasingly important in event planning. Technology now allows for immediate responses to attendee concerns, making it possible to enhance the experience as the event unfolds. Mobile apps with integrated feedback features, interactive kiosks, or quick-response QR codes strategically placed around the venue can provide instant insights. Imagine an event app that prompts attendees to rate the inclusivity of a session immediately after it concludes, or a kiosk that gathers quick thoughts on the day's activities. This immediacy not only improves the current event but also provides data that can influence long-term planning.

Social Media Engagement

Harnessing the Power of Online Interaction: In the age of digital communication, social media platforms are invaluable for real-time feedback. Monitoring channels like Twitter, Instagram, and LinkedIn during your event can provide immediate insights into how attendees are engaging with your programming. Encouraging the use of a specific event hashtag can help consolidate this feedback, making it easier to respond and adapt. Engaging with attendees directly on these platforms demonstrates a commitment to inclusivity and responsiveness, key trends in the future of event planning.

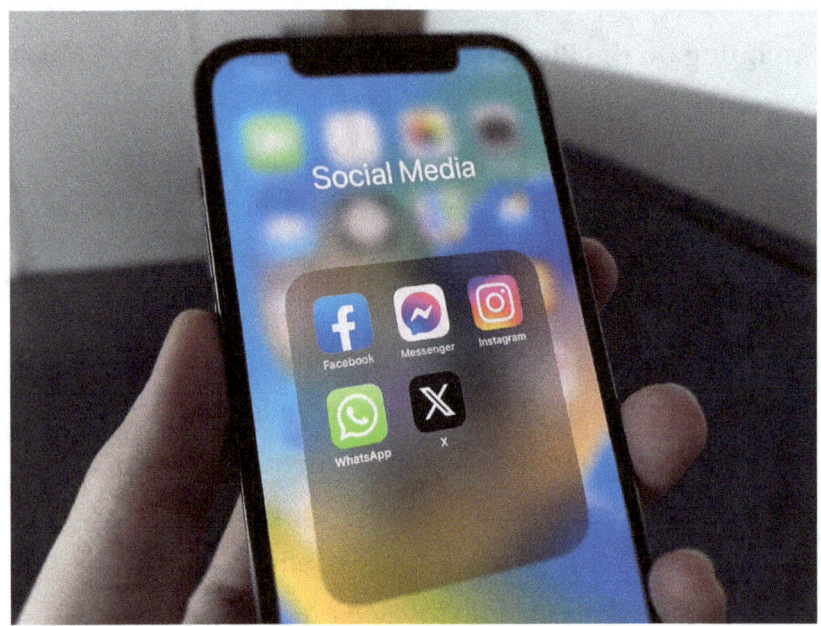

Follow-Up Interviews

Deepening Your Understanding: While surveys and real-time tools capture broad feedback, follow-up interviews offer a deeper dive into the attendee experience. By speaking directly with a diverse group of participants, event planners can gain nuanced insights that might not be evident in survey data alone. These interviews can explore how well the event met the needs of different attendee groups, from those who opted for non-alcoholic options to those requiring specific accessibility accommodations. As event planning continues to prioritize inclusivity, such personalized feedback will be crucial for making informed adjustments.

The Continuous Improvement Process

Building on Feedback: The feedback gathered should not simply be filed away but should serve as the foundation for ongoing improvements. Analyzing this data allows planners to identify actionable changes that can enhance future events. For instance, if attendees indicate that the variety of non-alcoholic beverages was limited, future events can expand their offerings to include a wider range of options. This process of continuous improvement ensures that each event is more inclusive and aligned with emerging trends than the last.

Transparent Communication: Closing the Feedback Loop

As we move toward a more inclusive future, transparent communication about how feedback is used is vital. Sharing the results of your feedback analysis and the steps being taken to improve future events not only builds trust with attendees but also reinforces your commitment to inclusivity. A post-event communication, such as a newsletter or social media update, that outlines key takeaways and planned enhancements shows attendees that their voices have been heard and valued.

Looking Ahead: Trends in Inclusivity and Sober Events

The future of event planning is one where inclusivity and sober-friendly practices are not just trends but are integral to the success of every gathering. By employing thoughtful feedback mechanisms and continuously evolving based on the insights gained, event planners can ensure that their events not only meet the current needs of their audiences but also anticipate and adapt to future shifts in attendee expectations.

Through these practices, you are positioning yourself and your events at the forefront of a movement that values diversity, accessibility, and meaningful connections, setting a new standard for inclusivity in the event planning industry.

Chapter 11

YOUR NEXT STEPS
Putting It All Together for a Successful Conference

The true measure of an event's success is not just in the knowledge shared or the business deals made, but in the way attendees feel as they walk away. Are they leaving inspired, connected, and energized, or are they heading home feeling depleted and overlooked?

In other words, did the meeting fill them up or did it fail them?

Modern event planning must aim to fill attendees up—to ensure that they depart with valuable insights, meaningful connections, and a profound sense of belonging.

The Power of Inclusivity in Event Planning

Consider the story of Sarah, a dedicated professional who had always felt out of place at networking events because she preferred not to drink. At a recent conference, she was pleasantly surprised to find a range of thoughtfully crafted non-alcoholic beverages and dedicated spaces for quieter conversations. For the first time, Sarah felt fully engaged in the evening activities, forming connections that were deeper and more meaningful. She left the event not only satisfied but also empowered, having participated in an environment that truly valued her preferences.

Then there's John, an industry veteran who had grown weary of the loud, high-energy networking events that left him drained by the end of the night. At an inclusive event focused on mindful engagement, John discovered a wellness lounge where attendees could relax, meditate, or enjoy a soothing tea. This thoughtful addition allowed him to recharge and connect with others in a calm, supportive setting. By the end of the event, John felt invigorated, not depleted, and he left with a renewed enthusiasm for his work and new professional relationships that would last well beyond the conference.

These stories illustrate the profound impact that inclusive practices can have on attendees. When event planners prioritize inclusivity—whether through sober options, diverse activities, or thoughtful layouts—they create environments where every participant feels valued, respected, and connected. This approach is not just about meeting basic needs; it's about enhancing the entire experience, ensuring that attendees leave feeling enriched rather than exhausted.

The Shift Towards Inclusivity

The move towards inclusivity in event planning is not just a trend; it is a necessary evolution in response to the diverse needs of today's professionals. As society increasingly values diversity, wellness, and mindful living, events that embrace these principles will not only stand out but will also foster deeper, more authentic connections among attendees.

Inclusive events are about more than just accommodating different needs—they are about celebrating diversity and creating spaces where every attendee, irrespective of their health, lifestyle choices, or personality, feels truly welcomed and valued. This shift requires event planners to rethink the traditional ways of organizing conferences and to embrace new approaches that prioritize the well-being and comfort of all participants.

Partnering with Sober Life Rocks

As you move forward in your journey to create more inclusive events, remember that you don't have to do it alone. At Sober Life Rocks, we are committed to helping professionals, event planners, and HR managers reimagine the way conferences and networking events are designed and attended. We understand the challenges you face and the pressures to meet diverse expectations, and we are here to offer a different perspective.

By partnering with Sober Life Rocks, you gain access to the tools, insights, and support needed to make your events not just inclusive, but truly transformative. Our expertise in creating environments that honor and celebrate sober choices helps foster a community where no one feels isolated. Imagine hosting an event where every attendee feels genuinely connected to a community that respects and values their choices. Moreover, for HR professionals, we offer a supportive community that you can introduce to your employees. This community can provide them with a network that celebrates and honors their sober choices, ensuring they have access to ongoing support both before, during and after events.

If you're ready to elevate your events or want to explore more about our community, we invite you to book a free discovery call with us. During this call, we'll discuss your specific needs and how we can collaborate to create events that make a meaningful impact. You can schedule your call by emailing laura@soberliferocks.com or by visiting our website, www.soberliferocks.com.

Additionally, if you're looking for a full list of alcohol-free drink recipes to enhance your event, don't hesitate to reach out. Together, we can ensure that your next event is one where every participant leaves feeling valued, uplifted, and ready to take on their next challenge with renewed energy. Let's make your next event one that fills attendees up rather than leaving them feeling drained.

Your Next Steps

As you consider the future of your events, ask yourself: Are you filling people up, or are you failing them? The choice is yours, but the rewards of choosing inclusivity are clear. By adopting these practices, you not only enhance the experience for your attendees but also contribute to a broader cultural shift towards inclusivity and wellness in professional settings.

Start by evaluating your current event planning strategies. Where can you incorporate more inclusive practices? How can you better cater to the diverse needs of your attendees? And most importantly, how can you ensure that every participant leaves your event feeling connected, respected, and fulfilled?

The journey towards more inclusive, sober-friendly events begins with a single step. Partner with experts who can guide you, engage with your audience to understand their needs, and continuously seek feedback to improve. Together, we can set a new standard in event planning—one that prioritizes connection, inclusivity, and the well-being of all attendees.

In conclusion, the future of event planning lies in embracing inclusivity. By making these changes, you're not just planning a conference—you're creating an experience that leaves a lasting impact. So, let's get started. Let's fill, not fail. Let's make every event a place where everyone feels they belong.

www.ingramcontent.com/pod-product-compliance
Lightning Source LLC
Chambersburg PA
CBHW071044240526
45471CB00014B/578